A Martian Wouldn't Say That

Compiled by
Leonard B. Stern
and Diane L. Robison

Illustrated by Saul David

PRICE STERN SLOAN, INC.
a member of
The Putnam Berkley Group, Inc.
New York

Published by Price Stern Sloan, Inc.
a member of
The Putnam Berkley Group, Inc.
200 Madison Avenue
New York, NY 10016

A Martian wouldn't say that : confidential memos TV executives wish they
hadn't written / compiled by Leonard B. Stern & Diane L. Robison.
    p.   cm.

    1. Television--Production and direction--Humor.   I. Stern,
Leonard B.   II. Robison, Diane L.
PN1992.75.M28   1994
791.45'0207--dc20   93-29572
ISBN 0-8431-3612-X   CIP

Printed in the United States of America

1 2 3 4 5 6 7 8 9 10

This book is printed on acid-free paper.

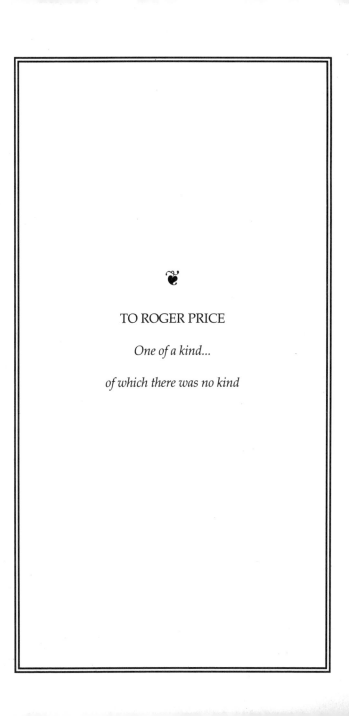

TO ROGER PRICE

One of a kind...

of which there was no kind

ACKNOWLEDGMENTS

Without Jimmie Komack this book might be without a title. It was he who received the rather mystifying note, "A Martian wouldn't say that," challenging the authenticity of his dialogue in a script he wrote for *My Favorite Martian*.

In the preparation of this collection we relied upon written notes or verifiable conversations. If it were not for my co-editor Diane Robison's remarkable detective feats in tracking down elusive material or, when the notes were verbally given, finding corroborating witnesses, we also might have been without a book.

We are indebted to Bill Blinn, David Dortort, Larry Gelbart, Bob Justman, Norman Lear, Gene Roddenberry and David Wolper, who established that even the brightest hear from the weirdest. We are equally indebted to Sherwood Schwartz, who drew upon experiences with *My Favorite Martian* and his years of shepherding *Gilligan's Island*, to fill in what might have been gaps in our research.

Very special thanks must go to E. Jack Neuman, who gave graciously of his archives and supplied us with enough material to fill several volumes. Grateful acknowledgment to Sam Denoff and Bruce Johnson who unknowingly shared identical mind-blowing rejections from two different sources, proving that absurdity knows no boundary. And for granting us access to his 'memo'rabilia, we send our warmest thanks to Gerald Gardner.

Nor must I forget to thank Sam Bobrick, Jim Brooks, Alan Burns, Merrit Malloy and Irma and Rocky Kalish for providing us with a steady flow of material. Our heartfelt thanks to Alan Spencer, our emissary to situation comedies, who vigorously researched contemporary inanities.

Completing the list of memo aficionados who also gave generously of their time, their documents and enthusiasm are: Steve Allen, Blue Andre, Danny Arnold, Donald Baer, Milton Berle, Peggy Chane, Jack Chertok, Lionel Chetwynd, Bob Christiansen, Bill Dana, Saul David, Jerry Davis, Jon Epstein, Bob Finkel, Charles FitzSimons, Joel Freeman, Ed Friendly, Chuck Fries, Terry Galanoy, Roger Gimbel, Tom Greene, Robert Guenette, Bruce Hart, Lawrence Hartstein, Shelly Herman, Douglas Heyes, Roy Huggins, Bernie Kahn, Hal Kanter, George Kirgo, Philip Krupp, David Levy, Stephen Lord, Jerry Ludwig, Nancy Malone, Garry Marshall, Allan Nadohl, Andrew Nicholls, Barry Oringer, John Rappaport, Gene Reynolds, Sam Rolfe, Philip Rose, Arnie Rosen, Rick Rosenberg, Stanley Ralph Ross, Stanley Rubin, Patricia Rust, Laura Sevier, Mel Sherer, Ron Silverman, Ira Skutch, Julie Stein, Sam Stranges, Arnie Sultan, George Sunga, Joan Twekesbury, and Renee Valente and Jack Wohl.

We owe a very special debt to Jo Morgan for helping to shape this book at the outset and for remaining steadfastly organized throughout long periods of creative chaos. And, of course, to Tiffany Young, who contributed substantially to the health, welfare and editing of this book.

PREFACE

All of us who are television producers, writers and directors have one thing in common. We receive more memos from network executives than we really care to count. I cheated; I counted. Once. In the five years *Get Smart* was on the air, I received 2,033 memos over the course of producing 138 shows. The majority came from Broadcast Standards (read Censors) whose job it is to determine what should and should not be watched by TV viewers. Their memos were generally constructive, occasionally dictatorial and, from time to time, actually humorous.

Another 600 or more memos—I stopped counting—came from an almost equal number of V.P.'s (there's always been a great turnover of executives at the networks) who were in charge of Current Programming. Arbitrarily intruding upon the creative process, their memos were unintentionally naive, consistently bizarre and often eminently quotable.

I sat down and wrote a brief article incorporating the best quotes which, of course, were the worst, and sent it off to *POV*, the Producers Guild magazine, where I had been published in the past. Almost immediately, I received the best rejection notice of my life. Diane Robison, the editor-in-chief, wrote, "This is more than an article. It's a book!"

Sensing there had to be other misguided missives piled up on the desks of fellow writers and producers, she encouraged me to seek them out. She also made the mistake of volunteering to help. Together we canvassed the creative community. Having assured anonymity, when desired, to both the memo's creator and recipient, we received enough mail, phone calls and faxes to start working on the book Diane had visualized. We hope the results herein give you as much enjoyment as the recipients of the original memos got when they opened their inter-office mail.

In the beginning there
was the word...

And a few days later
a memo to change it.

URGENT

TO: Bruce Johnson
FROM: VP, Development
RE: Pilot

We cast a black actor as our lead, but the way you've written the dialogue you can't tell that.

Memorandum

To: VP, Development
From: Bruce Johnson
Re: Pilot

That's what we intended!

URGENT

TO: Bruce Johnson
FROM: VP, Development
RE: Pilot

Okay, but how will the audience know he's black?

To: R.G.

We are convinced that your current episode is unwatchable. We'll have to run it in the summer.

Although Connie is a sociopath, make sure she's not without warmth.

FYI

In the original *Operation Petticoat* movie, a pet pig was used for great comic effect. In the rewrite for television, you eliminated the pig. Please reinsert. Remember, pigs are rating points.

Considering today's current sensibilities, when you discuss euthanasia be sure you do so in a positive light.

NOTES

It is too gruesome and unsympathetic to have Martin murdered while hooked up to life-support systems. Wait until he recovers, then kill him.

We have run the sequence of the barmaid serving drinks over and over and over. There is too much cleavage.

For Your Eyes Only

Please consider eliminating the child abuse and homosexual references. They are no longer popular with the audience.

Attention

As written, Howard is too sensitive — he's losing his predatory instincts. Please give him more of a salesman's soul.

In your current script, you attribute the quote, "Time is a great teacher, unfortunately it kills all its pupils," to Hector Berlioz. We do believe you are in error. Berlioz was a musician, not a writer.

Confidential

In this script, Beverly is described as "on top of everything." Please define "everything."

If you eliminate the Zippo lighter (no brand names), the immolation scene is acceptable.

Memo

In general, the coverage is excessive and our first cuts are running much too long. Please remember, *60 Minutes* is 48 minutes.

A question regarding Gertrude and Gerald, half-man, half-woman: Will he/she (or is it she/he) be half-stacked? If so, a half caution on her/his (his/her) costuming.

NOTES

This is the **best** script of *The Addams Family* we've read in a year. Attached are the notes for the **rewrite**.

MEMORANDUM

TO: E. Jack Neuman
FROM: Standards and Practices
RE: *Inside the Third Reich*

In the line, "And that little bastard in the big pants will strut across the stage wagging his mustache...," you must delete the word "bastard" in regards to Hitler!

MEMORANDUM

To: Standards and Practices
From: E. Jack Neuman
Re: Annotation that Hitler was a bastard

Hitler's mother was named Schicklgruber, and he was born out of wedlock. No less than two thousand prominent histories mentioned that fact, and no less than half the world's population — including his Holiness, Pope John — regards Hitler as a bastard.

MEMORANDUM

TO: E. Jack Neuman
FROM: Standards and Practices
RE: *Inside the Third Reich*

Okay, keep the "bastard."

21

Once you put a man in a dress, you can't reveal his pectorals.

To L.S.

Unfortunately, we are forced to put your program on hiatus. It has elements of quality for which we can't find an audience.

There are too many "hells" and "damns" in the first three episodes. Please spread them throughout the season.

Ca *ca* is unacceptable.
We suggest you change it
to, "My life is *doo doo*."

Please keep the point
of impact off camera when
"Maggie kicks Michael
in the groin."

Be sure not to show
the proctologist in action.

MEMORANDUM

TO: David Wolper
FROM: VP, Development
RE: Miniseries of Ulysses
The Iliad and The
Odyssey

Do you think the story will
hold up?

MEMO

To: VP, Development
From: David Wolper
Re: Miniseries of Ulysses

After weathering 3,000
years, I think the story will
hold up for one more
television season!

The view of Grecco's dead body in the mail cart should not be unnecessarily prolonged.

The celery may be construed as phallic. Use broccoli.

It is the opinion here at the network that your idea, on the whole, is probably not entirely without some possible merit.

You will have to re-edit the detonation of the land mine sequence. And please remember for all future episodes of *Tour of Duty*, we can only show a body coming down.

Is it possible to improve the caliber of writing without doing a disservice to the show's popularity and excellent demographics?

NOTES

If the writers had their way, they'd use "ass" on every page. Please limit them. How many asses do you think we can have on a network show?

To avoid sexual overtones, care should be exercised in the scene in which George pulls Martha down on the bed and rips her clothes off.

I think you're making a mistake having so many French involved in the production of *Les Misérables*.

MEMORANDUM

TO: Jerry Davis
FROM: VP, Current Programming
RE: Movie of the Week

Due to the sensitive nature of the script, we urge that this show be done in good taste.

FYI

TO:
FROM: VP, Current Programming
RE: Jerry Davis
Movie of the Week

Thanks for your memo. It arrived just in time as I was on the verge of doing the show in the worst possible taste.

Read At Once

I thought your memo
dated the 25th was vicious
and unnecessary. When
I want your opinion, I'll
give it to you.

Please obtain the
necessary legal clearance
before using the names
Cher, Oprah and Noriega.

$\mathbb{W}$e don't want to have problems with Broadcast Standards. Please eliminate the direction in your script which reads: "Offstage scream from a naked woman."

FROM THE DESK OF

Please consider changing Norton's occupation. You can't expect people to watch a sewer worker while they're having dinner.

MEMORANDUM

TO: The Producers

FROM: VP, Current Programming

RE: *The Fred Astaire Special*

Too much dancing.

At this time we don't think sodomy is a suitable subject for a *Movie of the Week*.

NOTES Trust me, your movie isn't as good as I think it is.

Acceptability of Joanne's vomiting will have to be determined when we see how it plays in the dailies.

The spontaneity of the show has been hurt by over-rehearsing.

Important

With the exception of Andrea's pedagogical speech on page 39, the inclusion of the long Clifford Odets quote on page 47 and the subsequent references to Homer and Ulysses, this rewrite is, by far, the least pretentious.

MEMORANDUM

TO: The Producers

FROM: VP, Current
        Programming

RE: *My Favorite Martian*

Please change the dialogue on Page 14. A Martian wouldn't say that.

Please do not sensationalize the dead gopher.

I know this is a reality based show — but why do we have to have so many unhappy endings?

On page 39, we can hear, but do not want to see, pigeon droppings.

Your argument is well taken. We agree there is more sexual explicitness on daytime soaps and also agree that the majority of a soap's audience is composed of housewives. What you fail to take into account is that, at night, these housewives become mothers.

NOTES

Regarding <u>He And She</u>, we want you to know this is the best show we've ever canceled.

❖ FYI ❖

To: Alan Spencer

From: VP, Development

Re: *Sledgehammer*

We need suspenseful music to underscore those two scenes.

❖ MEMO ❖

To: VP, Development

From: Alan Spencer

Re: *Sledgehammer*

Agreed. We should use something along the lines of Bernard Herrman's work.

❖ FYI ❖

To: Alan Spencer

Re: *Sledgehammer*

Bernard Herrman. Who's he? Never heard of him.

❖ MEMO ❖

From: Alan Spencer
Re: *Sledgehammer*

He composed the music for most of
Alfred Hitchcock's classic thrillers.

♣ FYI ♣

To: Alan Spencer
Re: *Sledgehammer*

Really? You mean like *Charade?*

❖ MEMO ❖

From: Alan Spencer
Re: *Sledgehammer*

Hitchcock didn't do *Charade.*

♣ FYI ♣

To: Alan Spencer
Re: *Sledgehammer*

But did Herrman?

❖ MEMO ❖

From: Alan Spencer
Re: *Sledgehammer*

Henry Mancini did the score for
Charade.

♣ FYI ♣

To: Alan Spencer
Re: *Sledgehammer*

Jesus, I feel like I'm playing *Trivial
Pursuit®.* Let's just hire this Bernard
Herrman guy to do the music, all right?

❖ MEMO ❖

From: Alan Spencer
Re: *Sledgehammer*

We can't! He passed away over a
decade ago.

♣ FYI ♣

To: Alan Spencer
Re: *Sledgehammer*

Then for chrissakes, why are we
even talking about him? Get Mancini!!!
I know he's alive. I saw him on a radio
commercial the other day.

We remind you once again, you cannot trivialize death on Sunday nights.

Dear Tony,

Admittedly, *Call Me Back* is a one-man show and a tour de force for Art Carney, but we still believe there are far too many monologues.

Please disregard the notes we were unable to send you.

You finally have a beginning, a middle and an end–but, unfortunately, not in that order.

In your rewrite, you've succeeded in obfuscating the story line with the plot.

To: Pearl Buck

From: VP, Development

Re: Script about the Bible

There's nothing of interest here.

"Sluts" is an improvement but still unacceptable.

We've cut the joke about the man who was experimenting with avocados but finally gave them up and went back to women. We find the whole idea tasteless.

Remember, our lead is an Indian. In the scenes in which he runs through the streets and across Central Park, make sure he runs appropriate to an Indian.

The reason your ratings are slipping on *Lou Grant* is that you're giving us *The New York Times*— we want *The Daily News!*

MEMORANDUM

TO: E. Jack Neuman
FROM: Broadcast Standards
RE: *Inside the
       Third Reich*

Please substitute Tessenow's
use of "horse's ass." Acceptable
alternatives would include
clown, buffoon, oaf and dunce,
among others.

MEMO

TO: Broadcast Standards
FROM: E. Jack Neuman
RE: *Inside the Third Reich*

Thanks, but none of these are as
good as plain, simple, direct old
"horse's ass."

49

In my opinion, a funny script, subject to the consensus of our comedy group.

The Sons of Italy are pressuring us to not have all the gangsters on *The Untouchables* portrayed as Italian. Could you change the name of Rocco Balboni to Seth Balboni?

Please remember that
style is more important
than dramatic coherence.

TO ALL CONCERNED:

From now on, eliminate
Roman numerals on any
cue cards. Undoubtedly,
this is why the line was
read "And now a few
nostalgic songs from World
War Eleven."

Can we make the rabbi less Jewish?

To avoid sponser conflict, please eliminate the line "He fell into a vat of facial lotion and softened to death."

TO: Arne Sultan
FROM: Standards and Practices
RE: *Get Smart*

When you depict the plunge of the knife into the back of the hunchback, do it tastefully.

Memorandum

TO: Standards and Practices
FROM: Arnie Sultan

It will be tastefully shot... our aim is to please.

TO: Arnie Sultan
FROM: Standards and Practices

Upon viewing yesterday's dailies, we feel the scene must be reshot. It would be better if the knife were to go into the part of his back which isn't hunched.

Make sure the psychiatrist doesn't appear incompetent. Many aren't.

Notes

How committed are you to this Oscar Wilde fellow? If you want him to do the first draft, it's all right with me.

Try to avoid controversy on *The Governor and J.J.* For example, on page 23, Governor Drinkwater vehemently attacks a southern senator, calling him a babbling nincompoop. Southerners are very sensitive as to how their representatives are portrayed. Could you pick another part of the country where this might not be true?

MEMORANDUM

TO: Stan Rubin
FROM: VP, Current Programming

While we realize that Anthony Quinn is playing a contemporary mayor of a southwestern city, and the show is issue-oriented, please refrain from stories about the poor, the old, radicals, chicanos or blacks.

You cite as your source for the Picasso quote in question, *The Zen Book*. Could we have a less esoteric reference?

To: The Writers

We're interested in your idea about a newly married couple and the ghost of the bride's first husband. However, having the ghost talk about things he can't do is disquieting. It reminds people that he's dead.

MEMORANDUM

TO: Tom Greene
FROM: VP, Current Programing

We understand what you are attempting...the message may be that beauty inside is more important and all that... but couldn't you just have the girl, as she's walking out of the cave, trip over a rock and discover a bag of diamonds or something?

MEMORANDUM

TO: VP, Current
         Programming
FROM: Tom Greene

Your suggestion would
destroy the message of
our story.

MEMORANDUM

TO: Tom Greene
FROM: VP, Current
         Programming

The viewers won't like it.
After all, you can't buy a
BMW with a message.

Important

Please change "the jeep is loaded and ready" to "the jeep is packed and ready" to avoid the implication of drinking.

To: S.T.

With the single exception of Seward's continuing to be excessively hostile throughout the script, the lack of a punch line for the second act, and the absence of a gratifying denouement speech, this is an excellent rewrite.

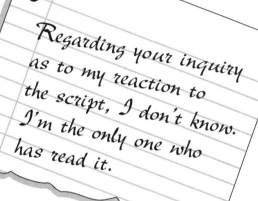

Regarding your inquiry as to my reaction to the script, I don't know. I'm the only one who has read it.

Mary's "Screw you, Larry" is still considered inappropriate.

This draft doesn't work. Unfortunately the script is strikingly similar to the material from which it was adapted.

We regret to inform you, we don't have any notes.

From the Desk of . . .

Try to get writers who have never written before.

The trading of the girl for the horse is unacceptable.

MEMORANDUM

TO: Larry Gelbart & Gene Reynolds

FROM: VP, Current Programming

RE: M.A.S.H.

Please clear your calendar for lunch on Friday. I need to explain how you guys keep screwing up M.A.S.H.

The license fee for the use of "Happy Birthday" is prohibitively expensive. Could Ralph celebrate Alice's birthday by singing "For He's a Jolly Good Woman"?

We're concerned about the uniforms on *Star Trek*. They look like the whole crew is wearing Dr. Dentons.

ATTENTION:

Please avoid anything morbid, inappropriate or detrimental to his image in the display of the dead, gay midget lying under the toilet.

This episode needs excitement. Where's the car chase? Remember, the car chase is as endemic to the genre as the adjective is to the English language.

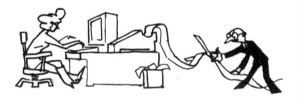

We must de-emphasize violence this season. Make the room red so the blood won't show.

We don't believe raising the level of music and drowning out the expletives works. What is said will be apparent to lip readers, and lip readers write the network.

Please clear the use of the name Princess Diana with her or her equivalent.

MEMORANDUM

To: Robert Guenette
From: VP, Development
Re: A documentary about the American Indian Family

We'd love to do such a picture but as we both know, not enough Indians have TV sets.

I am requesting you do something you've never done before — come in on budget.

URGENT

I know this is short notice but the network wants to see the script for the pilot <u>very</u> badly and <u>very</u> quickly. Is there any way you could write the script now and do the research later?

Too many "thees" and "thous" date the material.

When the nurses take a shower, do not have them nude.

The way the script is written, Ted's flatulence is too apparent...we suggest he belch instead.

MEMORANDUM

TO: Norman Lear
FROM: Broadcast Standards
RE: *All in the Family*

Since this segment deals with Meathead's impotence, when Meathead and his wife head for the stairs at the end of the script, you must fade out before they hit the stairs. We do not want to imply what they are going upstairs for.

For Your Immediate
Attention:

Could we please see another writing sample. The play you've submitted reads like a play.

To L.B.S.:

We're canceling *The Governor and J.J.* show as of the 17th of next month. That allows you four more episodes. Keep up the good work.

On page 7, Ed Norton says "va-va-va-voom." Before we can give clearance, what does it mean in English?

FYI

I've been on this job for 15 years and in that time I have read thousands of scripts and maybe 6 or 7 have been good – but yours, yours is the best I have ever read by far! The action is non-stop, the characters are beautifully delineated and track perfectly all the way through, the motivations are honest and real, each act break is organic and never feels manufactured to be a false ending for a commercial, the humor is witty, the arc of the story is flawless...

Unfortunately, all we're buying this year is crap.

You keep giving us profundities. We want jokes.

Although you've eliminated the discussed nudity and confined the lovemaking to under the sheets, we thought we could detect penetration.

memo

TO: Rick Rosenberg &
Bob Christiansen

FROM: Program Practices

RE: MOW, Gargoyles

Please be careful in depicting some of the more grotesque and terrifying scenes so as not to frighten the viewer.

The line, "It's a waste of time training eunuchs," could be offensive.

Do you have to show the dailies every day?

Whenever you use identical twins, please make sure we can tell them apart.

Dear E.A.,

I'm really excited by your new script. Those who have read it tell me it's exceptionally good!

ATTENTION

In the upcoming episode, please eliminate any unflattering reference to the Teamsters. We've yet to finish our negotiations with them.

TO: Jon Epstein
FROM: Standards and Practices
RE: *McMillan & Wife*
Opening Credits

The opening sequence bothers us. You have the camera following the actress from behind as she walks down a dark alley. We cannot see the fear in her face. We would prefer to see her walk toward the camera.

MEMORANDUM

TO: Standards and Practices
FROM: Jon Epstein
RE: *McMillan & Wife*

Can't be done. It would be too expensive to reshoot.

TO: Jon Epstein
FROM: Standards and Practices
RE: *McMillan & Wife*

You don't have to reshoot - just flip the film.

In these last few episodes, you've ruined what could have been a respectable failure with poor scripts.

On page 17, you refer to a female character as a person. This is an anachronism. In the fifties, a woman was not a person.

Please disregard our notes which were inadvertently sent to the wrong production company.

Please do not deliver scripts the day before you're shooting. We need time to praise and condemn them.

This season we are surfeited with shows which present normal, decent people in appealing situations.

NOTES

When Ralph says, "You're going to the moon, Alice," it may be the wrong destination. The moon is generally regarded as romantic. Could Ralph send her to Mars?

We cannot accept the script where an old shipmate of George's has become a woman, unless you provide a reasonable explanation.

We find this script excessively long and redundant. Why say the same thing over and over again? Repetition does a disservice to the effectiveness of the script. Less is always more.

Please
don't make
the tomato
too sad.

The bikini costumes
of the wrestlers must
prove adequate.

Skip the erudition.
This is not PBS.

MEMORANDUM

TO: Joseph Wambaugh
RE: Upcoming MOW

Regarding scene on page 38.
We don't think cops really
talk that way. Please correct.

To: Broadcast Standards
From: E.J.N.

In compliance with your annotation requirements, I have enclosed the annual reports of the U.S. Attorney General from 1972 through 1988. There is a Mafia.

You establish that your private detective is a former lawyer whose fee is twenty-five dollars an hour. No lawyer, not even an "ex," would work for that kind of money.

We're getting enormous pressure about gratuitous violence. Let's make a deal. You can put back the two punches to the head if you eliminate the explosion in the airport terminal.

In the scene where the thug is brutally beaten, please make sure that he is not a member of any minority group.

INTEROFFICE MEMO

TO: Executive Producer

RE: Pilot, *Hogan's Heroes*

Hogan's Heroes is the funniest pilot we have seen in months. Unfortunately, we must decline it. If the pilot is this good, how could you sustain it a second week?

Morbidity is not comedy. Please eliminate the line on page 26 which reads, "When you're seventy and you get up in the morning and don't feel any pain — you're dead."

In response to your list of suggested writers for your upcoming pilot: Who is Truman Capote?

We're most interested in a David Susskind televised special of *Hamlet*. Could we please see the script?

To Whom It May Concern:

Contradictory to the Producers Guild of America's position on gray listing, we do not practice age discrimination. Many of our writers are in their late thirties.

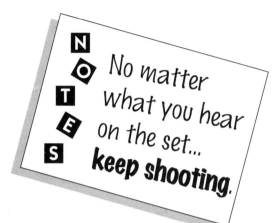

This will confirm that I have reviewed your revisions of the edit of the Corvette sequence. It is still unacceptable to have Rufus comment, as he drives past the Braille building with the lights off, "I guess they must be working tonight."

TO: VP, Current Programming

FROM: Gene Roddenberry,
          Executive Producer

RE: *Star Trek* Story Outlines

To be perfectly honest, your last letters had me sorely tempted to include here a request that you omit sending me copies of your future story comments. Your statement, "We must and will insist upon more novel material than we have accepted in the past," is misleading and totally unacceptable. You have gotten in the past and will continue to get some of the most imaginative and novel concepts in television writing today. If we are going to refer to the records, let's do so fully — including the fact that many of our most varied and most successful episodes were sent to script over your own strong objections.

This is not to say you have not been an excellent executive in your position. We have appreciated your help, talent and friendship. But let's establish again, at the beginning of this third season, that on a show as complex and difficult as *Star Trek*, the producer must produce the show.

We recognize NBC's several contractual rights regarding content, but we have no intention of permitting others to take over our contractual functions. We welcome comment, but no one here is going to sit quietly when we receive letters which seem to suggest that on the slender basis of a story outline you can guess all our plans and conversations about the story and can make the final omniscient decision that it will or will not translate into a good or varied script.

Your letters had all the earmarks of some form of "ultimatum," and if this does, in fact, reflect NBC thinking, I suggest you have the Head of Programming contact me immediately.

Further, I suggest you keep in mind that story outlines are, at best, rough blueprints of a script — they are a small part of the constant flow of communication between producer and writer, a working tool among storytelling professionals. If you want story outlines so finely rewritten and polished that every point is touched, every problem solved, every dramatic value totally realized and every possible doubt erased, then someone had better start petitioning NBC to run *Star Trek* in the next millennium.

–G.R.

Man is the only animal that blushes...
and needs to.

Man is the only animal that laughs...
and needs to.

The rest of the animal kingdom
is not in on the joke...
The rest of the animal kingdom and
a few network executives, that is.

GARRY MARSHALL
Paraphrasing Mark Twain upon
receiving the Lifetime Achievement Award
at the American Comedy Awards, 1990.